# NATURE'S FURY

# FLOOD!

ANITA GANERI

W
FRANKLIN WATTS
LONDON · SYDNEY

First published in 2006 by
Franklin Watts
338 Euston Road
London NW1 3BH

Franklin Watts Australia
Hachette Children's Books
Level 17/207 Kent St, Sydney, NSW 2000

Produced by Arcturus Publishing Limited,
26/27 Bickels Yard, 151-153 Bermondsey Street, London SE1 3HA

Editor: Alex Woolf
Designer: www.mindseyedesign.co.uk

Picture credits:
*Corbis*: cover and 8 (Reuters/Jayanta Shaw), 11 (George H. H. Huey), 12 (Alberto Pizzoli),
16 (Kjeld Duits/epa), 17 (Kapoor Baldev/Sygma), 18 (Alessandro della Bella/epa),
20 (Howard Davies), 22 (Sergey Ilnitsky/epa), 23 (Bettmann), 24 (Themba Hadebe/epa),
25 (John Gress/Reuters), 26 (Elvis Barukcic/epa), 29 (Alexandra Winkler/Reuters).
*NASA Visible Earth*: 9, 19 (Jacques Descloitres, MODIS Rapid Response Team,
NASA/GSFC).
*Rex Features*: 4 (Sipa Press), 5 (Stewart Cook), 10 (Sipa Press), 13 (Sipa Press), 15 (Sipa
Press), 21 (The Travel Library), 27 (Nicholas Bailey).
*Science Photo Library*: 6 (Gary Hincks), 7 (Wayne Lawler),
14 (Carlos Munoz-Yague/LDG/Eurelios), 28 (Paul Rapson).

Every attempt has been made to clear copyright. Should there be any
inadvertent omission, please apply to the publisher for rectification.

A CIP catalogue record for this book is available from the British Library

Dewey Decimal Classification Number: 5541.48' 9

ISBN-10 07496 6922 5
ISBN-13 9780749669225

Printed in China

# Contents

# What is a Flood?

A flood happens when water from a river or the sea covers dry land. But a flood is far more powerful than this description makes it sound. Heavy rains can turn gently flowing rivers into terrifying torrents that sweep across the landscape, submerging it under metres of muddy water. Powerful storms and giant waves can send seawater cascading over low-lying coasts, drowning towns, harbours and people.

▼ *Flooding in Meissen, Germany, in 2002. Heavy summer rains caused the River Elbe to overflow its banks and spread onto the surrounding land.*

## Killer floods

Floods kill more people than earthquakes, famines, volcanic eruptions and other natural disasters. Over the centuries, tens of millions of people have died in floods. A single, huge flood can bring catastrophe, killing millions of people. Floods are more frequent than other natural disasters and they cause as much damage to property as all other natural disasters put together. Fast-flowing floodwater washes away buildings, cars, trees and roads. Even stagnant floodwater damages buildings, electricity cables and other infrastructure. Floods also alter the landscape by eroding soil, carrying it away and dumping it elsewhere.

## Flood types

There are three main types of flood: river floods, flash floods and coastal floods. Most floods happen on rivers, when excess water overflows from a river onto flat land called the flood plain. The most devastating floods happen along the world's great rivers,

such as the Mississippi in the USA, the Ganges in India and the Huang Ho in China. Flash floods happen suddenly when intense rain falls over a small area. Coastal floods happen when storms and tsunamis raise the sea level above the level of the coast.

Despite being so destructive, floods can also bring benefits. The soil on river flood plains is extremely fertile, making them good places to grow crops. This is why millions of people around the world choose to live on flood plains, despite the risk from flooding.

◀ Car roofs poke above floodwater in New Orleans, USA. The flooding was caused by Hurricane Katrina in 2005.

 **CASE STUDY**

### The Biblical flood

In the Bible, God sends a great flood that covers the whole Earth. Only a man called Noah and his family survive. There are many other, similar legends of great floods. They may be based on a real flood that happened about five thousand years ago in modern-day Iraq, where archaeologists found a thick layer of sediment deposited by massive flooding.

# Flowing Rivers

Before looking at why floods happen on rivers, it is useful to understand how rivers flow. The water on Earth is constantly circulating between the oceans, the atmosphere and the land. This circulation of water is called the water cycle. Water evaporates into the atmosphere from the oceans and land in the form of water vapour. When the vapour rises and cools, it forms water droplets that fall as rain and other precipitation. Some of the rain forms rivers and flows back across the land to the sea.

▼ *The flow of water down a river (centre) is part of the water cycle. Most of this water starts out in the sea and then returns to the sea through the mouth of a river.*

## Soaking in and running off
Rain either soaks into the ground or flows across the ground, when it is called run-off. The amount of water that soaks in or runs off depends on the type of ground, how wet the ground is and how heavy the rain is. Water soaks into some soils faster than others. For example, it soaks quickly into sandy soil but very slowly into clay. If rain falls so heavily that not all of it can soak in, the surplus rain sits on top of the soil or runs off it, downhill. When the ground becomes saturated (soaked with water), all the rain runs off.

## Forming a flood plain
Run-off finds the easiest way downhill. It collects into streams and rivers. On hills and mountains, rivers erode V-shaped valleys into the landscape. The eroded soil and rock is washed

downstream. When the river reaches lowland areas, the river naturally meanders (bends) from side to side. Over time, the meandering river slowly cuts a wide valley. During floods, the whole valley fills with water. Some of the soil and rock transported by the river is deposited. It builds up layers to make the bottom of the valley flat. The flat area on each side of the river is called the flood plain.

## GROUNDWATER

Water that soaks into the ground is known as groundwater. It seeps slowly down through the ground, saturating the rock below. The top of the saturated layer is known as the water table. In places, groundwater comes out of the ground and forms springs. Many streams and rivers start at springs. It is groundwater from springs that keeps rivers flowing even after long spells of dry weather.

▲ *Meanders on the River Bynoe in Australia. The flat area around the river, known as the flood plain, is formed from soil and rock left after floods.*

# Flood Patterns

Rivers often flood at the same time each year. These seasonal floods are caused by high seasonal rainfall or by melting snow in major mountain ranges. Seasonal rains fall at different times of the year in different climates. In South Asia seasonal floods are caused by heavy summer rains. The amount of water flowing down rivers can increase by about twenty times during this wet season.

## One-off floods

Many rivers flood only every few years, when there is particularly heavy rain that lasts several days. These floods do not happen in a regular pattern. There may be floods for two years running after many flood-free years. The severity of a flood is measured by how often such a flood happens. A ten-year flood happens, on average, once every ten years. A hundred-year flood on the same river, which would happen on average every hundred years, would be far more serious.

▶ *These floods in the Indian town of Guwahati were caused by the monsoon rains of 2000. That year's monsoon also caused floods in Nepal, Bangladesh and Bhutan.*

A person living alongside this river would probably only experience such a serious flood once in their lifetime. Tropical cyclones also create one-off floods because they drop huge amounts of rain in a short time.

## Flood surges

A flood does not happen as soon as it starts to rain. It takes time for the water to find its way into rivers and to build up. Then a surge of floodwater moves down the river. At a particular point on a river the water level gradually rises, peaks and subsides again. It may take many hours or even days before the river floods further downstream, and there can be floods hundreds of kilometres from where the rain that caused the flood actually fell.

▲ *A tropical cyclone over the Indian Ocean. Cyclones only happen at certain times of year, but cause flooding on rivers and coasts.*

## CASE STUDY

### Floods in China

Southern China has a summer monsoon, when a large volume of rain falls in a few months. The area is drained by two enormous rivers, the Huang Ho (Yellow River) and the Chiang Jang (Yangtze). Monsoon floods happen regularly along these rivers. When the rains are heavier than normal, the flooding can be catastrophic. In 1931, the level of water in the Chiang Jang reached 29 metres above its average level. Flooding along the Chiang Jang and the Huang Ho caused nearly five million deaths.

# Flash Floods

Aflash flood is a sudden, short-lived flood. Most flash floods are caused by extremely heavy rainfall from slow-moving storm clouds. This causes a huge volume of water to land in one place in a short space of time. The water takes the quickest route downhill, which may be along a narrow valley or through a town or city.

▼ Torrential rains caused these flash floods in the streets of Istanbul, Turkey. It is easy to be washed off your feet in fast-flowing water like this.

## Storm clouds

The intense rain that causes flash floods comes from storm clouds that can be more than 10 kilometres tall. The clouds grow when warm, humid air rises. Inside the clouds, air swirls up and down, carrying water droplets with it. The droplets grow larger until they fall from the base of the cloud. Sometimes the whole cloud collapses, releasing hundreds of thousands of tonnes of water in a few minutes. This is known as a cloudburst.

## Where flash floods happen

Flash floods often happen on short rivers that are too small to cope with the sudden flow of large volumes of water. Flash floods also occur when intense rain falls onto waterlogged ground. But they can also happen on dry ground if the rain is heavy enough. This is how they happen in deserts. Flash floods can happen in towns and cities when the rain is so heavy that drains cannot carry it away fast enough. In built-up areas there is little soil for the rain to soak into. But flash floods are very localized. They can affect just a single stream or street.

## CASE STUDY

### Boscastle, 2004

In August 2004, the English seaside village of Boscastle was devastated by a flash flood. In the afternoon of a very warm day, a series of giant thunderstorms formed in the area. The storms dropped 75 millimetres of rain in just two hours. Two rivers carried the water into the village, forming a roaring torrent up to 3 metres deep in the streets. Houses were destroyed and cars swept out to sea, but luckily nobody was killed. Experts estimate that this sort of flood is only likely to happen in Boscastle every 400 years.

▲ *Intense rain can cause flash floods even in desert areas. This is a flash flood in the Valley of the Gods, Utah, USA.*

# Coastal Flooding

The land along many coasts is only a few metres above sea level. In some places it is actually below sea level, and the sea is held back by natural banks or artificial barriers. In these areas a rise in sea level can cause water to pour inland, causing severe flooding. The rise may be caused by storms and high winds combined with high tides, and also by tsunamis (see pages 14 and 15). Seawater can also flow up estuaries, causing flooding far inland.

## Storm surges

Most coastal flooding is caused by storm systems such as tropical cyclones. These cause a rise in water level called a storm surge. In a storm system the air pressure is lower than normal. In other words, the pressure of the air pushing down on that part of the Earth's surface is less than average. The lower air pressure allows the water underneath to bulge upwards slightly to form a storm surge. The highest storm surges are caused by tropical cyclones. They can be five metres high, or more.

▼ *The streets of Venice are regularly underwater at high tide in autumn, and during storms. Up to 65 per cent of the city becomes flooded.*

## Areas at risk

Low-lying coastal areas are often highly populated. Millions of people live in cities that could be affected by coastal flooding. Parts of some major cities, such as London, are only a few metres above sea level.

Low-lying islands can be completely submerged in a coastal flood. The Italian city of Venice is built on 120 small islands and the city regularly floods during storms. Twenty per cent of the Netherlands is below sea level. This land is made up of areas called polders. The polders have been reclaimed from the sea by surrounding them with banks called dykes and draining the water away.

▲ *Houses flooded up to their roofs in New Orleans. The water level rose only slowly as floodwater spread through the city.*

**CASE STUDY**

### New Orleans, 2005

In August 2005, the city of New Orleans on the south-east coast of the USA was badly flooded by the storm surge from Hurricane Katrina. The surge pushed seawater into a lake next to the city, raising its level 2 metres above normal. Levees (flood barriers) collapsed and the water flowed into the city, much of which is below sea level. Seventy-five per cent of New Orleans was flooded, some of it to a depth of 6 metres.

# Tsunami Flooding

*T*sunami is a Japanese word meaning 'harbour wave'. Tsunamis are sometimes called tidal waves, but they are nothing to do with tides. Tsunamis travel very quickly across oceans as low waves. But when a large tsunami reaches shore, it rears up and sweeps inland, devastating everything in its path.

### Triggering tsunamis

Tsunamis are usually caused by undersea earthquakes. If an earthquake causes the ocean floor to rise or fall suddenly, the water above falls into the hole or is pushed upwards. This movement sets off a tsunami on the ocean surface. Tsunamis are also triggered by undersea landslides and volcanic eruptions. In 1883, the gigantic eruption of Krakatau in Indonesia set off tsunamis up to 40 metres high that swept ashore on nearby islands.

▲ *This is a computer simulation of how a tsunami forms after a giant landslide under the sea. The landslide makes the water move either up or down.*

## How tsunamis travel

Once a tsunami is triggered, a series of waves spreads out in all directions, like ripples on a pond. They travel at more than 800 kilometres per hour – as fast as a jet airliner. The waves are only a few metres high, but the gap between one wave crest and the next can be hundreds of kilometres. When the waves reach shallow water, they slow down, increase in height and get closer together. The waves gradually lose energy as they travel, but can reach coasts thousands of kilometres from where they are triggered. The first sign of an approaching tsunami is a dramatic drop in sea level, as though the tide has gone out very quickly and much further than normal. This is the first wave trough arriving. It is soon followed by giant waves breaking on the shore.

▲ *Devastation in part of the Indonesian city of Banda Aceh. The photograph was taken one day after the massive tsunami hit in 2004.*

## CASE STUDY

### Asian tsunami, 2004

On 26 December 2004, there was a huge earthquake under the Indian Ocean, near the island of Sumatra. It was the second most powerful earthquake ever recorded. The sea bed lifted suddenly by several metres, setting off a tsunami that hit the coastlines of Indonesia, Thailand, Sri Lanka and India. At sea, the waves were only half a metre high, but grew up to 30 metres high as they approached the shore. Low-lying parts of these coasts were devastated as the waves swept inland. Towns and villages were flattened. More than 283,000 people died.

# Human-made Floods

The vast majority of floods happen naturally, but sometimes people also cause floods. Most are accidental. They happen when stored water escapes from behind dams or embankments. In the future, climate change caused by global warming will also lead to more floods on rivers and coasts (see page 29). Human beings will be responsible for these floods because it is our use of fossil fuels that is the main cause of global warming.

*▼ This Japanese dam was broken by floodwaters from Typhoon Togake in 2004. The surge of water from the breaking dam would have made the flooding worse.*

## Dam bursts

We build dams on rivers to store water for water supply and irrigation, to produce hydroelectricity and also to prevent flooding (you can find out how dams prevent flooding on page 26). But in a few rare cases, dams designed for these jobs have collapsed, causing deadly floods in the valleys

below. Dams collapse because they are poorly designed, because they are damaged by powerful earthquakes, or because floodwater flows over the top of the dam, eroding the foundations at the base. Some experts believe that giant flood-control dams are disasters waiting to happen.

## Deliberate floods

Sometimes we flood land deliberately. For example, the land behind dams is flooded permanently by a reservoir. Dams stop the natural flow of water down a river, which can damage wildlife habitats along the river bank. On some rivers, dam sluices are opened occasionally to create floods downstream. The rush of water helps to maintain the habitats. Floods have also been used as weapons of war. In 1938, Chinese soldiers broke dykes along the Huang Ho River, causing flooding that stopped a Japanese invasion. In 1943, British bombers broke two dams in Germany, flooding an important industrial area.

▲ *These people were forced to leave their homes because their villages were to be flooded by dams along the River Narmada in India.*

## CASE STUDY

### St Francis Dam failure, 1928

The St Francis Dam in California, USA, was completed in 1926. It was built to supply water to the city of Los Angeles. The reservoir was filled in 1928. Cracks soon appeared in the concrete, but engineers were not concerned because they thought the dam was still structurally sound. A few days later, the dam collapsed. A wall of water 38 metres high crashed down the valley and through several towns. More than 400 people died. Last-minute design changes, unstable rock and poorly mixed concrete all contributed to the disaster.

# Effects on the Landscape

Floods change the shape of the landscape along rivers and coasts. During a flood, erosion increases and rivers carry and deposit more sediment. Erosion cuts into the river bed and banks, and sediment is dropped on the flood plain. Floods can even cause a river to change course completely by cutting a new channel.

### Erosion

Fast-flowing floodwater has incredible power. It picks up rocks and pushes them along. The rocks crash into the river bed and banks, eroding them even more. In flash floods, huge boulders can be washed downstream. In steep valleys the erosion weakens the valley sides, causing landslides and mudslides. In very dry areas, where the soil is loose, torrential summer rain cuts deep gullies into the landscape.

▶ *This house was lucky to survive when erosion by a flash flood in Switzerland in 2005 undermined other buildings on the same street.*

## Deposition

During a flood, river water turns brown because of the huge amount of sediment it is carrying. Some of this sediment settles on the river bed, making it more shallow. When river water flows over a flood plain, it drops sediment, covering the plain in silt or mud. Deposited sediment can also build up natural embankments on the riverside. When the river reaches the sea, sediment is deposited, forming a delta.

## Effects on vegetation

Floodwater rips some plants out of the ground and strips the leaves and branches from others. Flash floods and tsunamis have the power to snap tree trunks and pull their roots from the ground. Plants die if they are submerged by floodwater for several days. When coasts flood, seawater soaks into the ground and its salt kills some plants. In desert areas, however, floods allow seeds that have been lying dormant in the soil for years to germinate and bloom.

▲ *An area of desert in Australia, seen from space. The green areas are places where plants have grown after flooding caused by summer rains.*

### VEGETATION STOPS EROSION

Plants help to reduce the amount of run-off from the land. Their roots allow water to soak into the soil. Roots also take up some of the water, helping to dry out the soil. Some water that lands on plants evaporates back into the air. Where vegetation is cleared, heavy rain runs off the land as soon as it falls, causing flash floods that strip away the loose soil.

# Living with Floods

Hundreds of millions of people live on flood plains and in coastal areas that are at risk from flooding. Why do people live in flood-risk areas, and how do floods affect their lives? In some countries people have no choice but to live with the threat of floods, because the only land available to them is on a flood plain. But there are also definite advantages to living in flood-risk areas.

▶ *When floods come, these houses in Bangladesh stay above the floodwater because they are built on tall stilts.*

### Good for growing

The main advantage of living on flood plains is that they are good places for growing crops. The sediment deposited on flood plains during floods is rich in the minerals that plants need, and every flood brings a fresh supply. The river is also convenient for irrigating the crops. However, when floods do come, they can destroy a whole year's crop.

## Wet rice farming

For centuries, rice farmers in Asia have relied on floods along huge rivers such as the Ganges and Mekong. Rice is a type of grass. It grows best in fields that are flooded for part of the year. The fields, called paddies, have earth banks around them. During monsoon floods the floodwater fills the paddies. The earth banks ensure that the floodwater remains there.

## More advantages

Cities have grown up alongside rivers because rivers provide water and transport. In developed countries people enjoy living alongside rivers because the river bank is a pleasant place to be, and they can fish and go boating. In developing countries many people live on low-lying coasts because they make their living by fishing at sea.

▲ *Farmers plant rice in paddies in the north of Vietnam. This method of farming would not be possible without regular floods.*

## CASE STUDY

### Flooding in Bangladesh

Bangladesh lies in an area of the world hit by regular river flooding and tropical cyclones. Eighty per cent of the country is made up of the flood plains and deltas of three huge rivers: the Ganges, the Brahmaputra and the Meghna. Millions of farmers live in these flood-prone areas. In 1991, a cyclone with a 6-metre storm surge hit Bangladesh, causing severe flooding and high winds. About 140,000 people died, 1.5 million homes were lost, and millions of tonnes of crops were ruined.

# Effects of Flooding

How does flooding affect people? When a flood strikes, the immediate danger people face is drowning in deep or fast-flowing water. Danger to life is much greater in flash floods and tsunamis when there is little or no warning. In tsunamis, people are swept inland as the floodwater washes in, then out to sea as the water washes out again. People are also injured by fast-moving debris. The effects of flooding are felt more severely in developing countries, which are often not prepared for major floods.

▼ *The kitchen of a flooded home in Kemerovo, Russia. Even shallow floodwater like this can cause severe damage to a property.*

## Property damage

Fast-flowing torrents of water can smash through buildings and wash them away. They can also erode the earth under buildings, making them collapse. Wooden buildings may simply float away. Even if floodwater rises gently, buildings are severely damaged by the water, which soaks into plaster and decorations. Furniture and other contents are damaged beyond repair by dirty floodwater. Despite their weight, cars float and are often washed away and wrecked. Coastal flooding also wrecks boats, which are lifted and carried inland. When floodwater finally recedes, floors are covered with stinking mud and debris. In 1966, severe flooding in the Italian city of Florence left historic paintings, books, buildings and sculptures damaged or destroyed.

## Infrastructure damage

Fast-flowing water sweeps away bridges by weakening their supports or pushing them over. Roads are damaged or their surfaces are washed away as water finds its way underneath and lifts the surface up. Beneath the ground, electricity mains, communications cables and gas pipes are also flooded.

Leaking gas mains and live cables become an additional problem. Water pours into basements, subways and service tunnels. Drains and sewers fill with water and overflow into the streets, causing a major health hazard.

▲ *Half-submerged trains in the town of Wilkes-Barre, Pennsylvania, USA. It can take weeks to get trains moving again after damage to tracks and rolling stock.*

## AGRICULTURAL DAMAGE

Flooding in rural areas is a major problem in developing countries. Small-scale farmers lose crops, animals, seeds for growing new crops, and any food stored from previous harvests. Irrigation systems can also be damaged. Most poor farmers have no insurance, and their families are left with nothing. The loss of crops can lead to poverty, hunger and malnutrition. In small countries that rely on agriculture for exports, flooding can lead to economic disaster.

# Rescue and Recovery

▼ *The armed services often help out during serious floods. This South African Navy sailor is carrying a child to safety from the swollen Zambezi River.*

The first task for the emergency services during a flood is to rescue people from the water. It is also important to rescue people from their cars, which can sink, trapping the occupants. Half the people killed in flash floods in the USA, for example, die in their cars. People trapped in the upper storeys of buildings, on roofs, in trees and on patches of high ground need to be rescued quickly if floodwaters are still rising.

## Finding shelter

People who have been rescued, and others who have abandoned their homes, must be given shelter, food and drink until the water goes down and they can return home. In developing countries the authorities may be overwhelmed. In such cases, aid agencies step in to provide shelter. Aid agencies also help in the long term when crops are damaged and there is danger of starvation. Floods often cause water supplies to be contaminated with sewage. Drinking contaminated water causes diseases such as typhoid, dysentery and cholera, so supplying clean drinking water is essential.

## Cleaning up

Once floodwaters start to recede, the clean-up operation can begin. Water must be pumped back into rivers from low-lying areas because it will not drain away naturally. This is especially important in hot countries, where stagnant water becomes a breeding ground for malaria-carrying mosquitoes. Damaged houses must be repaired and redecorated. It can be many months before people can move back home.

## CASE STUDY

### Rescue in New Orleans

When New Orleans was flooded by the storm surge of Hurricane Katrina in 2005, thousands of people were left trapped on their roofs, in hotels and other buildings, including the Superdome sports stadium. Despite the USA being one of the world's richest nations, it was four days before a large-scale rescue effort was put into operation and relief supplies arrived in the city. The national government and local officials were heavily criticized for their poor planning and communication. Hundreds of people lost their lives. Many would have been saved by a faster response.

▲ *Firefighters in the town of Gurnee, Illinois, USA, deliver materials for cleaning and repairing a shop after floodwater had been pumped out.*

# Flood Protection

For thousands of years people have been trying to protect their homes and crops from floods. Today there are two main methods of flood protection. We can build structures that stop water escaping from rivers or spreading inland from the coast. We can also reduce the amount of water flowing down a river, so that the water is less likely to overflow.

▲ *Floodwater being released through the Modrac dam in Bosnia and Hercegovina, to prevent the reservoir from flooding upstream.*

## Embankments

The simplest form of river flood protection is an embankment or wall on each bank of the river. This stops floodwater from overflowing onto the flood plain. These embankments are also called levees, from the French word for 'raised'. Water that would cause floods further downstream can be diverted along channels into other rivers or into hollows to form temporary lakes. Water can also be allowed to spread onto parts of the flood plain to stop it overflowing in other places. Temporary flood barriers can be made by piling up sandbags.

## Delaying the flood

Dams are sometimes built to prevent rivers from flooding. The reservoir behind the dam stores the rush of floodwater from upstream and releases it slowly, preventing a surge downstream. The level of water in the reservoir must be carefully managed so that floodwater does not make the reservoir overflow.

## Coastal flood protection

Low-lying coastal land is protected from storm surges by embankments, called dykes, and dam-like structures called barrages. A barrage is built across an estuary. Its gates are normally left open to let river water flow out to sea, but they close to stop storm surges from moving inland up the estuary. Reclaimed land in the Netherlands is protected by a line of dykes and barrages hundreds of kilometres long.

▲ *The Thames Flood Barrier in east London. Its gates close to prevent storm surges from flowing up the Thames to low-lying areas of the city.*

 **PROTECT OR NOT?**

Some flood experts argue that flood protection is a bad idea. Stopping a river from overflowing onto its flood plain simply pushes more water downstream, making flooding more likely there. Flood protection also encourages people to build houses on flood plains, which could be dangerous if a really large flood comes along. These experts say we should work *with* nature rather than against it.

# Flood Prediction

Predicting when floods are likely to happen is as important as flood protection. Accurate predictions allow floodwaters to be managed, give the authorities time to prepare for flooding, and enable people to be evacuated in good time. We can predict when rivers are likely to overflow their banks, when heavy rain is likely to cause flash floods, and when storm surges or tsunamis are likely to arrive.

▲ *A scientist measures a river's water level. This shows how floodwater is moving downstream.*

## Monitoring conditions

Weather forecasting is vital for flood prediction. An accurate forecast tells us how much rain is likely to fall, and where. The amount of rain that actually falls is measured with rain gauges. This data is combined with information about how saturated the ground is, about water levels along the river, about the area of land drained by the river, and the size of the river channel itself. All the data is fed into computers that calculate the likely water levels along the river over the next few days.

## Flood warnings

The information from computer models is used to issue flood warnings on television, radio and on websites. Different levels of warning tell people how serious flooding is likely to be. A low-level warning is given if minor flooding is possible. A high-level warning is given when serious flooding is inevitable. Warnings of flash floods are given when extra-heavy, localized rain is expected.

## Coastal flood prediction

Meteorologists keep track of tropical cyclones so that they can predict where they are likely to reach land. They also estimate the height of the storm surge so that the extent of flooding can be estimated. The Pacific Tsunami Warning System uses satellites and sensors at sea to detect tsunamis travelling across the ocean. A similar system is being developed for the Indian Ocean after the devastating tsunami of 2004.

## GLOBAL WARMING AND FLOODING

The Earth's climate is changing because of an increase in the overall temperature of the Earth's atmosphere, known as global warming. Global warming is making sea levels rise around the world because ice caps are melting, causing the oceans to expand. Global warming also appears to be making tropical cyclones more frequent. So coastal flooding is likely to become more frequent and more severe in the next few decades.

▲ *Lines are often marked on buildings and bridges to show the level of water during a flood. These lines are an easy way of seeing how deep floods have been in the past.*

## TEN OF THE DEADLIEST FLOODS

| WHEN | WHERE | WHY | CASUALTIES |
|---|---|---|---|
| 1931 | China | river flood | about 3 million |
| 1959 | China | river flood | about 2 million |
| 1970 | Bangladesh | cyclone | about 500,000 |
| 1939 | China | river flood | about 500,000 |
| 2004 | South Asia | tsunami | 283,000 |
| 1991 | Bangladesh | cyclone | 130,000 |
| 1815 | Indonesia | tsunami | 90,000 |
| 1883 | Indonesia | tsunami | 36,000 |
| 1963 | Italy | dam overtopped | 2,000 |
| 1953 | Netherlands | storm surge | 1,487 |

## GLOSSARY

**barrage** An artificial barrier across a river that is closed to stop a tidal surge flowing inland.

**cholera** A disease caused by bacteria in dirty water, that causes diarrhoea and vomiting.

**delta** A fan-shaped area of land formed by sediment where a river meets the sea.

**dormant** Inactive, but not dead.

**dyke** An earth bank along a river or coast designed to stop water flooding the land.

**dysentery** An infection of the intestines caused by micro-organisms in dirty water, that causes diarrhoea and stomach pain.

**erode** Wear away.

**estuary** The final section of a large river, where fresh water from the river mixes with sea water.

**evaporate** Turn from liquid to vapour.

**fossil fuels** Fuels formed from the remains of animals and plants that lived millions of years ago.

**germinate** Begin growing from a seed into a plant.

**humid** Containing a high amount of water vapour.

**hydroelectricity** Electricity generated by turbines that are powered by flowing water.

**infrastructure** Roads, bridges, railways, sewerage systems and other large public structures.

**irrigation** The supply of water to farmland for watering crops.

**levee** An artificial embankment built alongside a river to prevent flooding of the surrounding land.

**malaria** A disease carried by mosquitoes, which breed in stagnant water.

**meander** A long, looping bend of a river across its flood plain.

**meteorologist** A scientist who studies the weather.

**monsoon** A pattern of weather that brings a period of heavy rain.

**polder** An area of land reclaimed from the sea.

**precipitation** Rain, sleet, snow or hail.

**rain gauge** An instrument that measures the amount of rain that falls.

**satellite** A spacecraft that orbits the Earth.

**saturated** Containing so much water that no more can be soaked up.

**sediment** Small pieces of rock carried down a river by flowing water.

**silt** Sediment made up of very tiny pieces of rock.

**tropical cyclone** An intense storm system that develops over the ocean. Hurricanes are tropical cyclones.

**tsunami** A wave caused by an earthquake, volcanic explosion or landslide.

**typhoid** An infection of the digestive system spread by insects.

**vapour** Matter in its gas form.

## FURTHER INFORMATION

### Books

*Atlas of the World's Worst Natural Disasters* by Lesley Newson (Dorling Kindersley, 1998).

*Awesome Forces of Nature: Raging Floods* by Richard and Louise Spilsbury (Heinemann, 2003).

*Fire and Flood* by Nicola Barber (Ticktock Publishing, 1999).

*Our Violent Earth: Floods* by Nicola Barber (Wayland, 2001).

### Websites

www.environment-agency.gov.uk/subjects/flood/
Information on flood risks and advice on flooding.

www.geoprojects.co.uk/Keyfile/KeyBoscastle.htm
Report and photographs of Boscastle flash flood.

www.wwltv.com/sharedcontent/breakingnews/slideshow/083005_dmnkatrina/1.html
Slideshow of photographs of flooding in New Orleans.

geology.com/articles/tsunami-map.shtml
Maps and before-and-after photographs of the 2004 Asian tsunami.

www.pbs.org/wgbh/nova/orleans/proo-nf.html
Case studies and photographs of how cities are protected from floods.

www.geol.ucsb.edu/faculty/sylvester/Teton%20Dam/welcome_dam.html
Information, photographs and video of the Teton Dam failure.

# INDEX

Page numbers in **bold** refer to illustrations.